Making Sense of: Estate Planning

Plan ❖ Preserve ❖ Protect

Bryan E. Spencer

SECURE PUBLISHING, LLC

Making Sense of: Estate Planning
Plan ❖ Preserve ❖ Protect

Secure Publishing, LLC
2565 West Maple Road
Troy, MI 48084

The information contained in this book is not intended to be comprehensive and should not be construed to be individual legal advice for its readers. The laws pertaining to estate planning are complex and fluid. Therefore, readers should consult with an experienced team of Estate Planning Professionals for specific advice regarding their individual estate planning needs.

Printed in the United States
ISBN: 978-1-4675-3395-9

Dear Reader:

My personal experiences with my grandparents and great-grandparents are what directed my interest in the fields of financial and estate planning and are the foundation for the career path that I have chosen.

Due to my personal and professional experiences, I am able to write this book and share my financial and estate planning knowledge with you. I am writing from a non-attorney perspective and this book is not intended as legal advice.

I strongly urge you to seek out competent financial and legal counsel to address your personal situation. While it may seem intimidating to work with financial and legal professionals, I can guarantee you that there is no substitute for the knowledge and advice experienced advisors can provide to you and your family.

Please use this as a guide throughout your financial and estate planning journey and feel free to share it with your advisors and their team to assist them in addressing your specific needs.

Best Regards,

About This Book

This introductory book is intended as a guide and resource to probate and estate planning. The topics covered present a general approach and provides facts to consider as you begin the estate-planning process. As you read through the chapters, you will understand that proper estate planning requires not only an experienced and competent attorney, but also accounting, financial, and insurance professionals for an all-encompassing approach.

Your attorney will ensure that you have all of the appropriate documentation to establish the foundation of your estate plan.

Accounting professionals will ensure that you are currently maximizing your tax deductions and continue to maximize your returns in the future.

Financial professionals assess your investments to ensure that they are properly aligned with your financial goals and also assist you in establishing a long-term plan to maximize asset growth and security for you and future generations. Financial professionals play a major role in the "funding" of a trust when one is included in a comprehensive estate plan.

Insurance professionals will review insurance coverage on your life, home, and automobiles to safeguard your estate from the unexpected.

This Book is For You if:

You want . . .

> to avoid unnecessary taxes . . .

You desire . . .

> to keep control of your estate . . .

You wish . . .

> to keep your estate out of probate . . .

You need . . .

> an overview of estate planning tools.

CONTENTS

CHAPTER 1

Estate-Planning Options

---

*I*t is not uncommon for the average person to declare that the topic of estate planning evokes both emotional and fearful sentiments. Many individuals are uncomfortable talking about estate and financial planning as it pertains to "what happens when I die," while others express the sentiment that their heirs will have to deal with what happens "after I'm gone." Such comments can be shortsighted, especially for people who have children and/or own property.

Many people mistakenly think that estate and financial planning are strictly for individuals who are wealthy. Nothing can be further from the truth (although some people believe spending money to put their financial house in order is too expensive).

Planning for your family's future is important. When determining what type of estate and financial plan would best suit you and your family, you should consider the emotional impact your decisions will have on a grieving family when you're gone.

Options

There are three primary options in estate planning: (1) doing nothing: (2) creating a will; or (3) creating a comprehensive estate plan, which may include the use of a revocable living trust. The following is a brief explanation of what occurs when implementing each plan:

Doing Nothing (Intestate)

In the event a person passes away without any type of estate plan in writing, they are considered to have died *intestate.*  Assets that have no owner are submitted to a probate court to determine heirs. The court appoints a personal representative (executor) who gathers the estate's assets and assembles an inventory of items in the estate (for example: jewelry, automobiles, real estate, or family heirlooms). The personal representative is paid a fee for their time spent on administering the probate estate and is required to publish a Notice to Creditors with the county legal news (or the local newspaper), that requires unknown creditors to state their claim against the estate in a four month window of time.

Since the decedent has left no instructions for the distribution of the estate, the court applies State law to determine the identity of the heirs of the estate. The court will then direct the personal representative to distribute the estate according to what the legislature has determined to be the wishes of the "average person." In the event that the person has no living relatives to claim the assets in the probate estate, the assets will revert to the state.

> If you do not leave instructions, probate court applies State Law to determine your heirs.

Creating a Will

A familiar option in estate planning is a will. A will is a legal document whereby a person nominates a personal representative who makes final arrangements, appoints the guardian or conservator of minor children, distributes personal property and represents the estate in probate court. Anyone of sound mind and of the age of majority (18 years old, in most states) can establish a will. A will must be proved valid in court for its terms to be enforced. The probate court determines if a will is valid by examining the form of the document and verifying that the signatures on the document are valid and were not obtained through fraud, duress or undue influence.

> A will must be proved to be valid to be enforced and the probate court determines validity of your statement of last wishes.

If a will is found to be in proper form and is uncontested, the court will enforce the terms of the will and allow the personal representative to distribute the decedent's assets as stated in the will.

If a will is not in proper form (for example: the signatures are invalid, there is a question about capacity or coercion, or a creditor, beneficiary, and/or third party contests the will) the probate court will then conduct a formal supervised review to determine the true intent of the decedent. In the event that the probate court, after reviewing evidence presented, determines that a will is invalid, the will is dismissed, and the estate is distributed as if the decedent died *intestate.*

Because probate can be a time-consuming and expensive process, it is obvious that doing nothing to secure their families' future can actually cost time and money and take an emotional toll on surviving family members and other heirs.

The Probate Process

Probate is the legal process by which non-titled property from an estate is transferred to the heirs of a deceased person or persons (either named in a will or determined by the probate court). In Latin, the word *probate* means to prove. Probate is a public process in which the contents of an estate are available for review by creditors and/or beneficiaries.

Estates often linger in probate for six to eighteen months,[1] depending on whether the deceased died *intestate*, the complexity of the estate, and the backlog of cases before the probate court. There are six basic steps in the probate process:

> - ***Validating the Will.*** A probate judge will determine if a will is valid. Sometimes, even a seemingly well-prepared will may be declared invalid if the document does not meet all necessary laws and requirements. If a will is

---

[1] AARP Report "Wills and Trusts"

declared invalid, the probate court will then direct the personal representative to distribute the estate according to the rules of *intestate succession.*

- **Notifying all Parties.** Once a typical probate estate is opened, the decedent's creditors, heirs, and potential beneficiaries are informed of the decedent's death. In most states, unknown creditors have four months to make a claim against the estate.[2] This is an opportunity for anyone who believes that they may have an interest in the estate to come forward and make a claim.

- **Taking Inventory.** The property and personal belongings subject to probate must have a value assigned to each item. An appraiser and/or accountant may need to be hired to determine the value of the decedent's property and accounts. Once filed with the court, the inventory is open to review by the public, unless the personal representative requests that the inventory is returned after the court's inventory fee is determined.[3]

---

[2] MCL 700.7606(1)
[3] MCL 700.3301

- ***Paying Debts.*** The decedent's debts that are determined to be valid are settled from the estate. In some cases, it may be necessary for the probate court to determine the validity of debts.

- ***Paying Taxes***. For each year that an estate remains open, the court-appointed personal representative must file state and federal income tax returns on behalf of the estate. Any estate and inheritance taxes are paid from the estate prior to distribution to the beneficiaries.

- ***Distribution to Heirs and Beneficiaries***. After all debts, administrative expenses, elections made by the surviving spouse and/or family, taxes, and other charges are settled, the heirs and beneficiaries receive their portion of the estate as dictated by the validated will.

Monetary Costs of Probate

As you can imagine, the six steps we just covered include their own set of costs and fees. Additionally, unless an estate qualifies for "small estate" or affidavit proceedings (for estates valued at under

$21,000 after the payment of funeral and burial expenses), an attorney will generally need to be retained and paid to assist in the settlement of a decedent's estate. Common legal fees include, but are not limited to:

- **Initial Filing Fees**: A fee assessed by the probate court to file the paperwork necessary to open an estate.

- **Publication Fee:** Once a personal representative has been appointed for an estate, that person must publish a Notice to Creditors of the decedent's death in the county legal news (or in some instances, the local newspaper).[4]

- **Inventory Fee:** A fee collected by the probate court, based on the total value of the property subject to probate.

- **Annual Accountings:** Annual accounts are required to be filed with the probate court every year that an estate remains open.

- **Estate Tax Preparation Fees**: For every year that an estate remains open, federal and state income taxes must be prepared and filed.

---

[4] MCL 700.3801

Emotional Costs of Probate

Every step in the probate process requires divulging information about the decedent and the decedent's holdings in a very public forum. When a person dies *intestate*,

assets or personal property, such as a favorite piece of jewelry or other memento, may not be distributed to the intended recipient causing hard feelings and disharmony among family members.

Creating a Comprehensive Estate Plan

An estate plan typically consists of multiple instruments that are drafted to cover an array of possibilities and estate-planning options. These documents are tailored to fit the needs of individual clients and their families. Most comprehensive estate plans include documentation that will allow clients to avoid both living and death probate (covered in Chapter 3), appoint guardians/conservators, have "catch-all" provisions for forgotten assets, as well as planning options to distribute assets and personal property after death. These documents will be discussed in greater detail in later chapters.

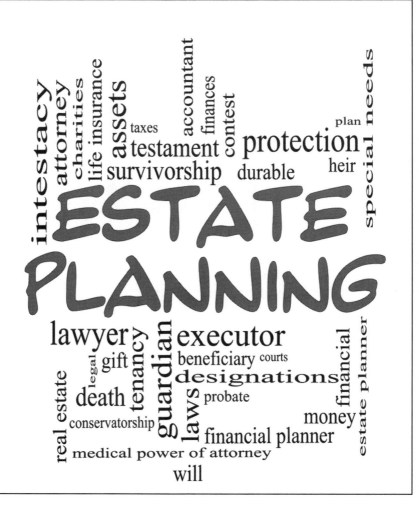

CHAPTER 2

What You Should Know About Wills vs. Trusts

Chapter Overview
- What is a Revocable Living Trust?
- Differences Between Wills and Trusts
- Other Types of Trusts
- Situations When a Trust is a Must

---

*A*s discussed in the previous chapter, many consider there to be three main options when it comes to estate planning. The previous chapter provided an overview of the difference between doing nothing and creating a will—steps that may involve the probate process. This chapter will compare and contrast simple wills and the basic revocable living trust.

What Is a Revocable Living Trust?

A revocable living trust is a legal document that becomes effective upon execution. A revocable living trust survives the death of the executing parties (called settlors) and provides additional options that cannot be found in a will. Living trusts typically hold cash, real property, personal property, and investments for the benefit of others. which allows the settlors to place restrictions on distribution from the trust.

> A revocable living trust survives your death and provides additional options not found in a will.

Additionally, a revocable living trust can be changed throughout the settlors' lifetime but becomes irrevocable upon the demise of the last living settlor. Benefits to using a revocable living trust as part of your estate plan may include:

- ***Providing for Minor Children***. When minor children are involved, it is important to protect their interests until they reach the age of majority. A revocable living trust will manage assets on your children's behalf until they are adults and will provide for their financial needs no matter who is appointed as their guardian.

- **Minimizing Taxes.** Certain trusts are implemented to mitigate, and in some instances completely alleviate, Federal Estate Taxes for those who are subject to the tax.

- **Protecting Your Privacy.** A revocable living trust is a "private" document that does not become part of the public record, unless you wish to file it with the county in which you reside.

- **Increasing Protection from Creditors.** A specific clause in revocable living trusts called the "spendthrift provision" limits the access that creditors can have to the assets you allocate to a beneficiary. This protection lasts as long as the assets are managed by a trustee who has the complete discretion to determine when and for what amount to distribute to the beneficiary.

Differences Between Wills and Trusts

Creating a will increases protection from dying *intestate.* Establishing a revocable living trust increases protection from a will. One main weakness of using a will is that you must die or become incapacitated in order for it to become effective. A will itself will not protect you from living probate or keep matters of your estate private the way a comprehensive estate plan will.

A simple way to illustrate the differences between wills and trusts is to review them side-by-side in the following table:

	WITH A WILL	WITH A TRUST
ESTATE & FAMILY COSTS	For a will to have legal effect, it must be validated by a probate judge.	When drafted and funded properly, a trust allows an estate to avoid the probate process.
Financial Expenses	Taxes, attorney's fees and probate fees, (such as the probate inventory fee, as well as accounting, appraisal, auction, personal representative, and advertising fees) are all part of probating a will.	Because a trust allows an estate to be transferred without the probate process, the family suffers no financial loss from probate expenses. Trust and estate-planning services cost a fraction of the probate fees assessed to persons who only have a will.
Delays	State law requires estates in probate to remain open for a period of time. During that time, anyone wishing to file claims on the estate may do so.	Without court involvement, trusts are generally easier and less time-consuming to settle.
Privacy	To have any legal authority, a will must be proved valid in probate court. When a family probates a will, the document itself, the worth of the estate, and the contents of the estate all become public record. The result is anyone may review or purchase copies of an estate's probate file.	Trusts are private family documents. Even if proof of a trust's existence is recorded, information on the contents and worth of the estate, how it is divided and to whom it is distributed, all remain confidential.
Control	When a will is submitted to probate, a judge makes the final determination on who distributes the estate, who receives the assets, and how those assets are divided if there are challenges to the will or the will is unclear.	The settlors, or creators of a revocable living trust, determine the party controlling the estate, who is known as the "trustee." The settlors also determine the beneficiaries of the trust, the persons who will receive the proceeds from their estate.

Other Types of Trusts

Revocable living trusts are not the only trust documents that may be used as part of a comprehensive estate plan. Other types of trusts include:

- ***Retirement Asset or Stretch IRA Trusts***. A trust that is funded with qualified retirement assets such as traditional IRA's or employer provided plans (Ex/ 401K, 403(b) 457). The main purpose of this trust is to force a beneficiary to take required minimum distributions over their life expectancy from the retirement assets held by the trust rather than allowing them to pull the entire value out of the plan in a lump sum. This plan will result in tax deferred growth over the life of the beneficiary and will significantly reduce income taxes.

- ***Charitable Trusts***. A name given to several types of irrevocable trusts that are usually drafted to allow either the income or proceeds of the estate to be distributed either directly to an IRS-defined charitable beneficiary upon the death of the trust grantor/settlor or in installment payments until the trust is exhausted.

- ***Supplemental Income Trusts.*** A supplemental income trust (Amenities Trust) is implemented when a trust beneficiary is receiving (or likely will be eligible in the future to receive) need based government benefits such as Medicaid or SSI, and a direct inheritance would disqualify them from receiving benefits. This type of trust is structured to allow for the maximum benefit from assistance plans while still allowing a beneficiary to receive distributions for amenities from the trust.

- ***QTIP-QDOT Trusts.*** Qualified Terminable Interest Property Trusts and Qualifies Domestic Trusts are typically drafted in blended family situations and situations where one spouse is not a citizen of the United States, respectively. QTIP's decrease the ability of the surviving spouse to disinherit the children of the first spouse to die. QDOT's postpone the payment of the Federal Estate Tax (for families over the Federal Estate Tax Exemption limit) until the death of the surviving spouse.

- ***Spendthrift Trusts.*** Spendthrift trusts are provisions within another trust (such as a revocable living trust) that limit distributions to beneficiaries over a fixed period of time or until a qualifying event occurs (for example graduating from college; being substance abuse free for a set period of time; or successfully passing a drug test). The settlor is able to define the qualifying events and/or distribution amounts while he or she is still living, and the successor trustee of the trust is legally bound to carry out those provisions.

- ***ILIT/SOS Trusts.*** Irrevocable Life Insurance Trusts and Single Owned Survivorship Trusts are advanced tax planning Trusts that provide liquidity to an estate while removing the death benefit of the life insurance from the Settlors/Grantor's gross estate.

- ***Education/Support Trusts.*** An education or support trust can be used to allow the settlor(s) to distribute assets specifically for the education or support of one or more beneficiaries. The settlor(s) determines exactly what is or is not covered under the trust.

- **_SBO Trusts_.** SBO trusts, or "solely for the benefit of" trusts, are irrevocable trusts that hold assets

> A SBO Trust is an essential tool in advanced Medicaid

for the benefit of a spouse or another designated individual. This trust is used as part of an advanced Medicaid plan and can make assets, which would otherwise be countable for Medicaid purposes, unavailable to be counted against your total maximum Medicaid benefit.

Situations When a Trust is a Must

There are times when no matter how detailed a will is, it still cannot offer the safeguards and protections of a trust. A well-drafted comprehensive estate plan will address any contingencies that may occur during your lifetime. These contingencies may include any of the following:

- **Minor Children.** A trust provides you with the opportunity to make provisions for the management of estate shares for minor children well into adulthood. The trust creator (Settlor/Grantor) is able to specify what their estate shares could be used for and how funds would be invested and allocated for the children's continued support, education, and overall growth. A will allows you to appoint a guardian and conservator for your children, but both of these positions are supervised by the court and result in reoccurring expenses.

- **Special Needs Children.** Children with special needs can be provided for through a supplemental income trust as mentioned earlier in this chapter. You cannot take advantage of the benefits of a supplemental income trust with only a will unless the will creates a supplemental income trust after your death and the administration of your probate estate.

- **Spendthrift Children.** Children who have difficulty managing money, who are not mature enough to manage their own estate share, who have substance abuse problems, or who have other personal issues can have their shares managed by the trust estate for a specific period of time or until a specified event has occurred.

- **Blended Families.** In situations where there are blended households, a revocable living trust will allow the heads of the blended households to make provisions regarding their individual assets and distributions to their children and family members. Proper estate planning can make sure that one spouse does not disinherit the children or beneficiaries from distributions from the other spouse's

> Proper estate planning can make sure that one spouse does not disinherit the children or beneficiaries from distributions from the other spouse's estate.

estate. Joint assets can also be allocated and distributed to each spouse's beneficiaries with minimal effort.

- **Generational Property.** If your family owns a multi-generational property, provisions can be made to allow that property to pass on to one or more generations  through the management of the property in your trust.

- **Honorary Trust Provisions.** An honorary trust allows for the care of cemetery plots or pets after a settlor's death. The most common use of an honorary trust is through a pet trust, which has provisions that allow you to provide for a non-human loved one, such as a horse, dog, or cat, after your death. An honorary trust allows you to appoint a caretaker for your pet, establish a standard of care during your pet's lifetime, and allocate a set amount of money to be used for the care and comfort of your pet. Any money left over (after the demise of your pet) is given to the caretaker you have appointed for their time and efforts on your behalf.

- ***Out-of-State Property.*** Probate may be required for every property that you own out of state, and it would be required separately in each state where you own property. Using a comprehensive estate plan would allow you to gather these properties into a trust and eliminate the need for probate in each state.

- ***Major or Chronic Illness.*** A recent major illness or chronic illness should force you to consider comprehensive estate planning. Proper planning will significantly reduce the need for probate, through the use of documents such as powers of attorney and living trusts.

- ***Family in Multiple States***. If you have family in multiple states, comprehensive estate planning is a great way to not only summarize your holdings but also to minimize the number of trips that may be necessary to settle your estate.

CHAPTER 3

If You Can't Make the Decision

- Financial Power of Attorney
- Advanced Health Care Directives

*W*hat happens when the time comes where you cannot make decisions on your own? Who will manage your finances and make sure your bills are paid? Who will make sure that you receive the health care that you need? Essential documents in a comprehensive estate plan include powers of attorney and advanced directives to help you answer those questions and avoid living probate.

Power of Attorney for Financial Matters

A document in which a principal (you) appoint an "attorney-in-fact" (agent) to take responsibility for your financial holdings, pay your bills, and assist a designated patient advocate, when necessary, with

25

procuring a residence for you if you no longer can manage your own home. You can also specify exactly what assets and responsibilities are covered under your financial power of attorney.

Financial powers of attorney can be temporary or limited (for use during a short period of time to accomplish a specific directive while competent) or can be durable (intended for use during an extended time of incompetency until competence returns or death occurs). Additionally a financial power of attorney can be effective immediately or its effectiveness can be delayed until you are determined to be incapable of handling your own affairs.

> Financial Powers of Attorney can come in different forms and can become effective for different specified events or times.

In a typical Power of attorney incompetency of the principal is determined through the evaluation of two unrelated medical professionals (usually one physician and one psychologist if mental competency is at question or two physicians if physical capability is in question). Lack of competency will make a *durable* financial power of attorney effective.

Careful consideration must be given to whom you appoint as your financial power of attorney. You will be granting a significant amount of power and a broad scope of ability to your agent at a time where you may not be able to retract the powers that you have granted. Be sure that the person you appoint will follow the directives that you have set forth and will not abuse the power that you have granted to him or her.

Advanced Health Care Directives

Advanced health care directives are a set of documents where the patient (you) appoints a patient advocate to implement the health care decisions you have made if you are later unable to do so yourself.

> A Patient Advocate Implements health care decisions that you have already put in place.

The documents usually include a health care power of attorney, and an acceptance of patient advocate and HIPAA (privacy) waivers. In their entirety, not only does this set of documents allow you to appoint someone you trust to follow your instructions regarding your care but the documents also allow you to plan for multiple contingencies that could affect both your medical and physical care.

CHAPTER 4

What is Included in a Comprehensive Estate Plan

Chapter Overview
- General Legal Documentation Required
- What is Funding?
- How Proper Insurance can Protect Your Estate
- Tax Review/Tax Planning for Asset Preservation
- Importance of a Professional Estate-Planning Team

---

*I*n the previous chapters we reviewed different estate planning options and some of the topics that should be taken into consideration when you are deciding what type of plan would be most beneficial for you and your family. In most cases, a comprehensive estate plan is the most effective estate-planning  tool to address all possible contingencies, preserve your assets for the benefit of yourself and future generations, and to avoid living probate. A comprehensive estate plan consists of several legal documents, the review and advice of a diverse team of professionals, and assessment of your particular situation to give you the information necessary to determine the most beneficial estate-planning vehicle for you and your family.

General Legal Documentation Required

There are typically five legal documents and four supporting documents that form the backbone of a comprehensive estate plan:

- ***Revocable Living Trust (RLT).*** As discussed in Chapter 2, a revocable living trust is a crucial component in a comprehensive estate plan. The most basic RLT will allow for minimal involvement in the probate process, limit potential challenges to your estate plan, protect distributions to your beneficiaries from creditors while those assets are held in trust, allow you to appoint successors to carry out your wishes, designate beneficiaries, gift specific property, create specific instructions for the distribution of your assets, and protect minor or incapacitated beneficiaries.

- ***Certificate of Trust.*** A certificate of trust is a short-form summary of your revocable living trust. It includes the name and date of the trust, who created the trust, whether the trust is revocable or irrevocable, who you have nominated as your successor trustees, the applicable law for your trust and lists the trustee powers. Most financial institutions will require a copy of this document when you begin funding your trust. This document provides the minimal amount of information required while leaving the majority of your estate undisclosed and private.

- *Financial Power of Attorney.* As discussed in Chapter 3, a financial power of attorney should be implemented to avoid living probate if you are physically or mentally unable to conduct your banking, investing, or general financial transactions. The agent you appoint will ensure your bills are paid, that your accounts remain stable, and will work with your designated patient advocate in cases where you may need to reside in an assisted living facility.

- *Advanced Healthcare Directives.* As discussed in Chapter 3, advanced health care directives are essential to avoid living probate. The appointment of trusted individuals who can carry out your wishes is a critical component of your estate planning.

- **Pour-Over Will.** A pour-over will is a set of directions appointing your personal representative and directing a probate court to transfer your assets into a revocable living trust in case you have not done so while living. A pour over will is also used to appoint guardians for minors or incapacitated adults in your care. However, use of a pour-over will does require filing the will with your county's probate court and paying filing fees. That is why it is of utmost importance that your estate plan is properly funded, which we will cover below.

> To avoid probate court entirely, it is of utmost importance that your estate plan is properly funded!

- **Assignment of personal effects.** A document that transfers your personal effects into a revocable living trust. Trusts and wills alike allow you to leave specific gifts of personal effects anytime during your life on specific gifts pages (or any separate writing) that are incorporated by reference in your trust. These documents allow you to allocate everything from a vehicle to your last pair of socks to a specific individual. You may have specific items such as jewelry or firearms that have sentimental value for the ones you love. On these specific gift pages or in the trust itself, you can specify that those items are allocated to the person who will find them the most meaningful or beneficial.

- *Final Instructions.* Finals instructions are intended to serve as a general overview of your holdings as well as information to guide your successor trustee and/or personal representative. Common information includes where your accounts are located, whether or not you have a safe deposit box, a description of assets that you may be holding for someone else, and any debts owed to you as of the date of your death. This section also has a place for you to make your last wishes known, from what type of service you would like, if any, to who should be notified of your death. Gathering all of this information in a central location will facilitate the ease of transfer to your intended heirs.

- ***Deeds and Ancillary Documents.*** For many individuals, the value of their real estate represents a significant portion of their net worth. Just like the rest of your assets, your home needs to be protected by your estate plan. Generally, your team of estate planning professionals will prepare deeds to transfer your property(ies) into your estate plan upon the demise of the last settlor. Most states also require ancillary documents such as property transfer affidavits to preserve tax exemptions at a local level.

- ***Asset Transfer Letters.*** Asset transfer letters act as a set of instructions to the financial institutions where you hold accounts, to help you position your assets so they are covered by your estate plan. This process is called "funding".

What is Funding?

Once the trust is executed, the next step is the funding process. Your legal documentation is the "lock box" used for the protection of your estate. Like any good lock box, it is the most effective if it is filled with items and assets that you wish to protect. Funding is the process used to transfer your assets into your lock box, protecting them from the probate process and reviewing those assets to maximize potential benefits to your heirs.

If a trust is to control assets during the life of the Grantor/Settlor, title to those assets need to be transferred to the trust. This may sound strange, but remember that the trust creator is the owner and primary beneficiary of the trust and therefore continues to control assets owned by the trust without any limitations. In no way does transferring assets into a trust restrict one's access to those assets or restrict their use or distribution. You retain total control. Common assets that are titled into a trust during the life of the trust creator are bank and credit union accounts, stocks, bonds, brokerage accounts and other non-qualified assets. The beneficiary on life insurance policies are typically changed to the trust to ensure that the death benefit it distributed in accordance with the directions set forth in the trust. Determinations concerning the transfer of these

assets should be made with the assistance of a financial advisor who will be able to guide the best placement of these assets for future distribution.

In some cases, a person may have several of the same type of account or have accounts where they are dissatisfied with an particular investment or product company and wish to make a change. Financial advisors should make recommendations to maximize not only your return but also suggest investments that will best suit the objectives and plans that you have set forth in your trust. Once a person has transferred assets into their trust, they should take steps to protect those assets while they are living.

How Proper Insurance can Protect Your Estate

The most well-planned and complex estate plans can be depleted through incomplete or underfunded insurance policies. In many cases, your largest asset will be your home and other real property. Therefore it is important that you are appropriately insured for fire, theft, and loss to preserve that asset for your family.

Additionally, proper liability coverage is critical to maintain in case someone has an accident or is hurt on your property, and that person attempts to sue you for medical fees and damages. Liability coverage will help ensure that you are not paying out of pocket for such expenses and that you are not put in a position where your home may need to be sold to satisfy those bills. Likewise, proper auto coverage will also protect your assets from potential loss due to an accident that causes either personal injury or property damage.

Tax Review/Tax Planning for Asset Preservation

Another important part of a comprehensive estate plan is to have your tax liabilities reviewed to maximize the credits and/or deductions that are available to you. Reviews may uncover past missed opportunities that might result in a higher amended return and, therefore, higher asset retention and benefit for you and your family. Additionally, tax planning to minimize future liabilities will allow you to preserve your estate and minimize the taxes that you would otherwise pay.

Importance of a Professional Estate-Planning Team

As you have read in the previous chapters, proper estate planning is a complex process that involves more than one professional discipline. A member of this team should be an attorney who has substantial estate planning experience.

Just as an attorney specializes in law, a financial services professional is integral in ensuring that your trust is properly funded. Your financial specialist should analyze your accounts to ensure they are working for your benefit and will help you realize your financial goals.

You will realize the most benefit from your tax planning if you use a CPA for this process. If you make sure that you have the proper professionals in place, you will have peace of mind in knowing that you are properly protected and in the hands of the best team of professionals who can carry out your wishes and assist your family at a difficult time.

CHAPTER 5

Estate-Planning Workbook

*T*his chapter serves as an estate-planning workbook to use as you evaluate your estate and estate-planning needs. Completing this workbook should take you a fair amount of time and may be used as a starting point for discussions with your family concerning the steps you are taking to protect them and your estate. Please feel free to add notebook pages if you run out of room for any particular topic.

Why go Through the Process of Collecting Information?

This workbook will serve as a centralized source for all the information that may be relevant to your estate. As you go through this chapter you may remember investments or family situations that may need to be addressed as part of your estate planning. This workbook may also be used by family members after you pass away as a road map to settling your estate.

Personal Information Worksheet

You	Your Spouse
Name: _____	Name: _____
SSN: _____	SSN: _____
Date of birth: _____	Date of birth: _____
Are you a U.S. citizen? ☐ Yes ☐ No	Are you a U.S. citizen? ☐ Yes ☐ No
First marriage? ☐ Yes ☐ No	First marriage? ☐ Yes ☐ No
Married to: _____	Married to: _____
Date of divorce/death: _____	Date of divorce/death: _____

Address: _____

      Telephone number: _____

      Cell phone number: _____

      Email address:_____

Your Children

Child #1

Name: _____ Date of birth: _____

      Child of: ☐ Both ☐ Mr. ☐ Mrs. ☐ Adopted

      Spouse: _____

Grandchild #1: _____ Date of birth: _____

Grandchild #2: _____ Date of birth: _____

Child #2

Name: _____ Date of birth: _____

      Child of: ☐ Both ☐ Mr. ☐ Mrs. ☐ Adopted

      Spouse: _____

Grandchild #1: _____ Date of birth: _____

Grandchild #2: _____ Date of birth: _____

Real Property Worksheet

Property #1

Address: _____

Classification: □ Marital home □ Vacation property □ Rental

Type of Property? □ Single Family □ Condo □ Duplex

Estimated home value: _____

Is there a mortgage on this property? □ Yes □ No

If yes, who holds the note? _____

Mortgage balance: _____

Property #2

Address: _____

Classification: □ Marital home □ Vacation property □ Rental

Type of Property? □ Single Family □ Condo □ Duplex

Estimated home value: _____

Is there a mortgage on this property? □ Yes □ No

If yes, who holds the note? _____

Mortgage balance: _____

Property #3

Address: _____

Classification: □ Marital home □ Vacation property □ Rental

Type of Property? □ Single Family □ Condo □ Duplex

Estimated home value: _____

Is there a mortgage on this property? □ Yes □ No

If yes, who holds the note? _____

Mortgage balance: _____

Assets

Car #1	Car #2
Year: _____ Value: _____	Year: _____ Value: _____
Make: _____ Model: _____	Make: _____ Model: _____
Lien Holder: _____	Lien Holder: _____

Art (list and describe any valuable art that you own):

Jewelry (list and describe any valuable jewelry that you own):

Antiques and Collectibles (list and describe any valuable antiques and collectibles that you own):

Financial Accounts

Account #: _____	Account #: _____
Bank: _____	Bank: _____
□ Checking □ Savings □ CD	□ Checking □ Savings □ CD
□ Money market	□ Money market
Names on the account: _____	Names on the account: _____
Account #: _____	Account #: _____
Bank: _____	Bank: _____
□ Checking □ Savings □ CD	□ Checking □ Savings □ CD
□ Money market	□ Money market
Names on the account: _____	Names on the account: _____

Financial Accounts (Continued)

IRAs and/or 401(k) Plans:
(include vested amount, total value, and plan administrator)

Profit Sharing Accounts:
(include vested amount, total value, and plan administrator)

Any Other Employee Benefit Plans:

43

Investment Worksheet

Investments			
	Broker	Account Number	Value
Stocks			
Bonds			
Mutual Funds			
Corporation, LLC or Partnership Interests			
Other Investments			

Insurance Worksheet

Life Insurance

You	Your Spouse
Name of company: _____	Name of company: _____
Address: _____	Address: _____
Policy #:	Policy #:
Amount of policy: _____	Amount of policy: _____
Cash value: _____	Cash value: _____
Loans against policy? □Yes □No	Loans against policy? □Yes □No
Amount of accidental death benefit:_____	Amount of accidental death benefit:_____
Owner: _____	Owner: _____
Beneficiaries:	Beneficiaries:

Group Insurance Benefits

Name of company: _____	Name of company: _____
Address: _____	Address: _____
Policy #:	Policy #:
Amount of policy: _____	Amount of policy: _____
Cash value: _____	Cash value: _____
Loans against policy? □Yes □No	Loans against policy? □Yes □No
Amount of accidental death benefit:_____	Amount of accidental death benefit:_____
Owner: _____	Owner: _____
Beneficiaries:	Beneficiaries:

Fiduciary Appointment Worksheets

Guardians

Guardians are appointed in the event that you are deceased and you leave behind minor children. Guardians will take physical custody of your children and will make all determinations about their care and schooling. You may designate a person or persons to be Guardians for your minor child(ren), but the final determination of fitness and viability will be made by the probate court.

Name *(in order of preference)*	Contact Information
First Successor:	
Second Successor:	
Third Successor:	

Trustee(s)

A trustee oversees the plans that you have put in place to manage assets and other gifts that you have designated for your beneficiaries. This might include administering sub-trusts, business management, real estate management, or other investments.

Name *(in order of preference)*	Contact Information
First Successor(s):	
Second Successor(s):	
Third Successor(s):	

Executor/Personal Representative

This person or persons becomes the administrator of your estate plan after you pass away. Administering your estate plan includes collecting your assets, paying taxes, and distributing your assets under the direction of the successor trustee of your estate plan. Frequently the executor and the trustee of an estate are the same person or persons.

[ ] Mark this box if your executor(s) are the same as your trustee(s)

Name *(in order of preference)*	Contact Information
First Successor(s):	
Second Successor(s):	
Third Successor(s):	

Durable Power of Attorney for Finance

The agent that is appointed in a power of attorney for finance document will manage your accounts, pay your bills, and/or collect payment on your behalf if you are physically or mentally incapable of doing so. Spouses are successors for each other unless there is a reason, such as incompetency or family issue, to negate that appointment. This power expires upon your death and the executor and/or trustee takes over.

Name *(in order of preference)*	Contact Information
First Successor(s):	
Second Successor(s):	
Third Successor(s):	

Durable Power of Attorney for Health Care

The patient advocate appointed in a power of attorney for health care document will follow your directives set forth regarding your care and medical treatment if you are unable to voice those decisions. Spouses are successors for each other unless there is a reason, such as incompetency or family issue, to negate that appointment. This power expires upon your death.

Name *(in order of preference)*	Contact Information
First Successor(s):	
Second Successor(s):	
Third Successor(s):	

Miscellaneous Estate-Planning Worksheets

Trusts

Please list the name, date, and location of any trusts that you have established on your behalf or trusts where you are named as either a fiduciary or beneficiary.

Trust Name	Date	Notes	Are You:
			☐ Settlor ☐ Fiduciary ☐ Beneficiary
			☐ Settlor ☐ Fiduciary ☐ Beneficiary
			☐ Settlor ☐ Fiduciary ☐ Beneficiary
			☐ Settlor ☐ Fiduciary ☐ Beneficiary

Future Inheritance

List any money, personal property, and/or real property that either you or anyone in your family anticipates receiving.

Inheritance	
Source	Asset/Amount

Liabilities

List any outstanding financial obligations that you currently have. If you have insurance to cover any of these liabilities also indicate that in this table.

Date of Valuation	Amount	Source	Notes

Your Estate Plan

How would you like to pass your assets to your heirs? Are there any provisions that you would like to discuss with a professional estate planner?

_____
_____
_____
_____
_____
_____
_____
_____
_____
_____
_____
_____
_____
_____
_____
_____
_____
_____
_____
_____

Glossary

ADMINISTRATION - Court supervised handling of an estate during the probate process.

ADMINISTRATOR - A person appointed by the court to manage your estate under two conditions: (1) if you die without a valid will or (2) if you don't name an executor.

ADVANCE HEALTH CARE DIRECTIVES - A comprehensive document that combines a durable power of attorney for health care with a living will.

ANCILLARY ADMINISTRATION - A probate proceeding in a state where you own property, but that property is not your primary residence.

CERTIFICATE OF TRUST - Sometimes called an "abstract of trust," it gives a brief description of your living trust. This document allows you to provide proof of your trust without revealing private information within the trust.

DURABLE FINANCIAL POWER OF ATTORNEY - A legal document that authorizes someone to make financial decisions on your behalf that is created while you are competent, which will continue to be valid if you become incapacitated or incompetent.

DURABLE MEDICAL POWER OF ATTORNEY - A power of attorney that authorizes someone you trust to make health-care decisions when you are unable to do so.

ESTATE – Assets and liabilities, real estate and personal property owned at the time of death.

ESTATE PLANNING - The process you go through to ensure that (1) your estate incurs the least taxes *possible;* and (2) your property passes to your beneficiaries with the least amount of delay, hassle, and expense.

EXECUTE - The act of signing (and in some cases notarizing) trust documents.

EXECUTOR(TRIX) OR PERSONAL REPRESENTATIVE - A person or an institution named in a valid will to carry out the instructions of the will.

FUNDING - The process of transferring property from your personal name into your revocable living trust Funding is the process that allows you to avoid probating your assets when done in conjunction with a revocable living trust.

HEIR - A person who is legally entitled to inherit property from a deceased individual.

INCAPACITATION – A medical and legal determination that an individual is unable to make decisions on his or her own behalf. This condition usually must be certified by two or more doctors or mental health specialists.

INCOME DISTRIBUTION - Type of estate distribution that only provides income from the settlors' assets to the named heirs of the trust and protects the principal of the trust for a certain period of time.

INTER VIVOS – Latin phrase that means "between the living" or "while living."

INTESTATE - Legal status of someone who dies without a will or other valid estate-planning instrument.

IRREVOCABLE TRUST - A trust that cannot be changed, once established, except by reformation.

JOINT TENANCY - A form of property ownership in which two or more people own property together in such a way that anyone of them can act as owners of the whole.

JOINT TENANCY WITH A RIGHT OF SURVIVORSHIP – A type of ownership in which two or more people own the same property, and when one joint tenant dies, full ownership passes automatically and completely to the surviving joint tenant(s).

LAST WILL AND TESTAMENT - An instrument whereby you make a declaration of how you want your financial assets and property to be distributed after your death.

LIVING TRUST – An estate-planning document that you draft during your lifetime. This document will hold title to your assets and name your successors, beneficiaries, and any special provisions that you care to include regarding the distribution of your personal property, real property, and financial accounts. This document survives the death of the settlors and is considered to be "living," therefore avoiding probate. A living trust "dies" once the settlors' estate is closed.

LIVING WILL - A document used to state your wishes about whether to use, withhold, or withdraw medical treatment, such as life support systems, when you become terminally ill. Most states now incorporate living will language as part of an advanced health care directive.

MARITAL DEDUCTION - Exempts from federal estate tax all property passing from one spouse to the other by reason of gift or death.

NON-PROBATE PROPERTY - Property with a named beneficiary, life insurance benefits, property held in joint tenancy with a right of survivorship, and property held in trust that are not subject to the probate process.

PER STIRPES - A Latin term that means your heirs will receive their share of an inheritance "by representation" if their immediate ancestor would have received it if he or she were still living.

PERSONAL PROPERTY – All property owned by a decedent that is not real property, mineral rights, or anything built on or attached to the land. It includes items such as automobiles, guns, jewelry, china, artwork, furniture, and clothing.

PERSONAL REPRESENTATIVE - The person named in a will or, after a hearing, by the probate court to represent an estate throughout the probate process.

POUR-OVER WILL – A legal document that acts as a catch-all for any asset that a decedent may have forgotten to transfer into his or her estate-planning documentation.

POWER OF APPOINTMENT - Power given to someone else to make decisions affecting disposition or distribution of a decedent's estate.

POWER OF ATTORNEY - A legal document in which the principal (the person executing the documents) assigns rights, duties, and responsibilities to another to act on the principal's behalf.

PROBATE - A complex legal process that includes determining the validity of a will, appointing an executor or personal representative, paying debts and taxes, identifying heirs and creditors, and distributing property according to the dictates of a valid will or according to statutory law in cases where a decedent dies *intestate*.

REVOCABLE LIVING TRUST - A legal document that takes effect once it is executed and that survives a decedent's death. It can be revoked, amended, or terminated at any time while the settlor(s) is alive.

REVOKE - To withdraw or cancel.

SETTLOR - The person or persons who create a trust. May also be called a *grantor* or *trustor*.

SPENDTHRIFT TRUST - A trust that is part of some estate plans (depending on family situations) that does not pay out all of its income until certain circumstances occur.

SPOUSAL GIFT – Most frequently used to protect a larger estate when one spouse's estate is much larger than the other spouse's estate.

SUCCESSOR TRUSTEE - Individual or institution appointed in a trust agreement who takes over management of trust assets upon the incapacity and/or demise of one or more settlors.

TENANCY IN COMMON - A type of joint ownership in which two or more persons own a single property. Each owner can dispose of his or her share of the property as well as pass it along separately at death without obtaining consent from other tenant(s).

TRUST - A legal document that establishes a legal entity that, in turn, is funded to hold assets for the benefit of specifically named beneficiaries.

TRUSTEE - Individual or institution appointed to manage a trust according to statutory law and under specific instructions set forth by the settlors of the trust.

61

When the Rich and Famous Failed to Plan

Sometimes no matter how much money you hav‹ cannot guarantee that you have the right protectio› and safeguards in place to successfully pass th maximum possible amount or your assets to you beneficiaries. On the next page there is a listing o famous individuals who failed to plan properly. No only did their families not receive all of the assets tha they should have received, the information about th estate became public because of a lack o comprehensive estate planning.

CELEBRITY ESTATE	GROSS ESTATE	SETTLEMENT COST	NET ESTATE	TOTAL LOSS
W.C. FIELDS	$884,680	$329,739	$554,887	37%
FRANKLIN D. ROOSEVELT	$1,940,999	$574,867	$1,366,132	30%
UMPHREY BOGART	$910,146	$274,234	$635,912	30%
HOWARD GOULD	$67,535,386	$52,549,682	$14,985,704	78%
WILLIAM E. BOEING	$22,386,158	$10,589,748	$11,796,410	47%
DEAN WITTER	$7,451,055	$1,830,717	$5,620,338	25%
ENRY J. KAISER, SR.	$5,597,772	$2,488,364	$3,109,408	44%
GARY COOPER	$4,498,985	$1,520,454	$3,454,531	31%
MYFORD IRVINE	$13,445,552	$6,012,685	$7,432,867	45%
WALT DISNEY	$23,004,851	$6,811,943	$16,192,908	30%
WILLIAM FRAWLEY	$92,446	$45,814	$46,632	49%
HEDDA HOPPER	$472,661	$165,982	$306,679	35%
MARILYN MONROE	$819,176	$448,750	$370,426	55%
ELVIS PRESLEY	$10,165,434	$7,374,635	$2,790,799	73%
J.P. MORGAN	$17,121,482	$11,893,691	$5,227,791	69%
JOHN D. ROCKEFELLER	$26,905,182	$17,124,988	$9,780,194	64%
ALWIN C. ERNST, CPA	$12,642,431	$7,124,112	$5,518,319	56%
FREDERICK VANDERBILT	$76,838,530	$42,846,112	$33,992,418	56%

PROBATE COSTS MADE THEM
"NOT-SO-RICH AND FAMOUS."

Updating Your Estate Plan

Congratulations if you have already established you estate plan! You should review your estate plan ever few years, or after a major life event such as:

- Divorce
- Death
- Marriage
- Change in employment
- Inheritance
- Other significant financial change
- Relocation to another state
- Sale or purchase of real estate
- Change in physical or mental ability of anyon named in your estate-planning documents
- Major estate-planning law or tax law changes

Notes

_____

_____

_____

_____

_____

_____

_____

_____

_____

_____

About the Author

Bryan E. Spencer is a founder of the Secure Group of companies located in Troy, Michigan, which include Secure Investors Group, Inc.; Secure Asset Management, LLC, a registered investment advisory firm; Secure Mortgage Funding, LLC; and Secure Tax Services, to provide clients with full service estate and financial planning.

Mr. Spencer has grown the business to a team of over 60 professionals who conduct business in multiple states, offering a diverse array of estate and financial planning services. He has been in the financial and estate-planning fields for 16 years and focuses on securing his clients' wealth both for their benefit and for future generations. His daughter, Scarlett, inspires him to assist others in their continued growth and well-being.

Additionally, Mr. Spencer has sat on the Board of Directors for multiple charitable foundations, including the Myasthenia Gravis Foundation and the 'SC Leadership Foundation.

A special thanks to Estate Planning Legal Services, PC, located in Troy, Michigan who has also contributed to this publication: Office Manager Amanda L. Murray, Attorney Paul Machesky, Attorney Steven G. Cozart and Attorney Joseph V. Coraci. The professionals at Estate Planning Legal Services, PC have decades of combined experience in estate and financial planning and have successfully prepared comprehensive estate plans for thousands of families.

Call And Let Us Help You
Secure Your Family's Future
(888) 692-0300